Content

Introduction

If you are wild about learning and wild about animals – this book is for you!

It will take you on a wild adventure, where you will practise key grammar and punctuation skills and explore the amazing world of animals along the way.

Each grammar and punctuation topic is introduced in a clear and simple way with lots of interesting activities to complete so that you can practise what you have learned.

Alongside every grammar and punctuation topic you will uncover fascinating facts about the world's rare and endangered animals. The reasons for animals going extinct today often involve people moving into their living areas or hunting and killing them.

When you have completed each topic, record the animals that you have seen and the skills that you have learned in the explorer's logbook on pages 44–45.

Good luck, explorer!

Slithery sentences

There are four 'species' of **sentence**:

A **statement** ⟶ gives **information**.

A **question** ⟶ needs an **answer**.

An **exclamation** ⟶ shows strong **emotion**.

A **command** ⟶ (without a subject) **tells** someone to do something.

We can also categorise sentences:

A **simple** sentence has just one clause (containing one subject and one verb):

The snake slithered by.

A **compound** sentence has two or more clauses joined with a coordinating conjunction. Each clause makes sense on its own:

The snake slithered by and the man jumped.

A **complex** sentence has a main clause (which makes sense on its own) and one or more subordinate clauses (which do not make sense on their own):

The snake, which moved swiftly through the forest, found its prey.

Task 1 Identify each type of sentence by writing S (statement), Q (question), C (command) or E (exclamation) in the box.

a A group of cobras is called a quiver. ☐

b Did you hear that growl? ☐

c Don't be afraid! ☐

d The cobra laid 50 eggs. ☐

e It's enormous! ☐

FACT FILE

Animal: King cobra

Habitat: The rainforests and plains of India, southern China and Southeast Asia

Weight: Up to 9 kg

Lifespan: Up to 20 years

Diet: Birds, fish, snakes, frogs, lizards and eggs

Task 2   Label these sentences simple, compound or complex.

a   King cobras build nests and they are very intelligent.   _____

b   Although they are shy, they will attack if provoked.   _____

c   Cobras are worshipped by Hindus.   _____

d   The snake growls if it feels threatened.   _____

Task 3   Add a subordinate clause beginning with **who** or **which** to these complex sentences.

a   The man, _____ ,
faced the king cobra.

b   The eggs, _____ ,
started shaking.

c   The children, _____ ,
enjoyed learning about snakes.

Exploring Further ...

Label these types of sentence.

Use S for statement, Q for question, E for exclamation and C for command.

a   Oh no!   ☐

b   What?   ☐

c   There's a cobra under that rock.   ☐

d   Stay very still.   ☐

Now slither to pages 44–45 to record what you have learned in your explorer's logbook.

Subject-verb agreement

Animal:	Sea lion
Habitat:	Oceans and seas around the world, except the Atlantic
Weight:	275 to 1000 kg
Lifespan:	20 to 30 years
Diet:	Squid, salmon, herring and mackerel

Sea lions love to float very close together in 'rafts'. They are in harmony! In the same way, **verbs** need to be in harmony or in **agreement** with their **subjects**.

Sea lions is endangered. **X**
Sea lions are endangered. ✓

Sea lions floats together. **X**
Sea lions float together. ✓

The **subject** of a sentence is **who** or **what** the sentence is about and it can be **singular** (a sea lion) or **plural** (two or more sea lions).

Task 1   Rewrite these sentences correctly so that the subject and verb agree.

a Baby sea lions is called pups.

Babby sea lions are called pups

b Sharks and killer whales loves to eat sea lions.

Shaarks and killer whales love to ead sea lions

c Sea lion are able to hold its breath for 20 minutes.

Sea lions are able to hold their breath sor 20 minutes

d Sea lions has earflaps, but seals don't.

Sea lions have earflaps bat seals don't.

Task 2   Fill in the gaps with the correct form of the verb 'to be'. Choose from the words in the fish.

 is   are   was   were

a The sea lion __was__ lying on the boat yesterday.

b The fishermen __were__ annoyed with the sea lions when they jumped aboard their boats.

c A shark __is__ a marine predator.

d Sea lions __are__ skilled at holding their breath for a long time.

WILD FACT

Sea lions love to relax and often rest aboard fishing boats. Sometimes the boats sink because the sea lions are so heavy!

Task 3   Put a circle around the correct verb form.

a The hungry killer whale devour / (devoured) the sea lion.

b A male sea lion are / (is) called a bull.

c The pup lie / (lies) on his mother.

d Sea lions (dive) / dives down to great depths.

WILD FACT

Sea lion pups are born on land and teach themselves to swim when they are about two weeks old.

Exploring Further ...

Write a sentence about the pictures below, making sure that your subject and verb agree.

The sea lion froze in complete terror when it saw the killer whale.

The mother sea lion was delighted to see her baby!

Now paddle to pages 44–45 to record what you have learned in your explorer's logbook.

Naming nouns

Nouns are naming words for a person, place, animal or thing. There are four types of nouns.

Common nouns name a general kind of person, animal, place or thing:

poacher   jungle   tusk

Collective nouns name groups of people, animals or things:

a tribe of natives   a herd of elephants

Abstract nouns name things that cannot be seen, heard, touched, smelt or tasted:

love   fear   sleep

Proper nouns name a particular person, place, time, event or organisation. They always start with a capital letter:

Charlie   India   World Wildlife Fund

FACT FILE

Animal:	Asian elephant
Habitat:	Southeast Asia
Weight:	2041 to 4990 kg
Lifespan:	Up to 60 years
Diet:	Tree bark, fruit, stems, roots and leaves

Task 1   Underline all the nouns in these sentences.

a Elephants are the largest mammals on land.

b Their trunks are used to tear down trees and pick up grass.

c Large herds are called clans.

d I was filled with joy when I saw the amazing animals.

Task 2

Sort these nouns into the appropriate column in the table.

herd   India   elephant   clan   anger   ivory   Asia   mammal
hope   mirror   Emily   Monday   crowd   hurt   flock   peace

Common	Proper	Collective	Abstract
Elephent	India	herd	anger
ivory	Asia	clan	hope
mammal	Emily	crowd	hurt
mirror	Monday	flock	peace

Task 3

Draw a line to join the clauses on the left with the correct nouns on the right.

Sadly, Asian elephants are endangered because:

a | their habitat is being destroyed to build   tusks, skin and meat.

b | poachers are hunting them to sell their   the timber industry.

c | they are captured and sent to work in   roads, houses and farms.

WILD FACT

Elephants flap their large, thin ears to try to stay cool. They use their powerful trunks to spray water on to their backs.

WILD FACT

Asian elephants live in grassy plains and forests. Females spend their entire lives in large groups called herds, but males leave the herd at 13 years old.

Exploring Further ...

Solve these clues.

a   These nouns cannot be seen   _Abstract_

b   These nouns name groups   _Collective_

c   These nouns name things   _Common_

d   These nouns name cities   _Proper_

e   A group of elephants   _Collective_

f   A long tooth by an elephant's nose   _Common_

Now stomp to pages 44–45 to record what you have learned in your explorer's logbook.

Exquisite adjectives

Adjectives are used to **describe** a noun or a pronoun.

The exquisite snow leopard is known for its beautiful, thick fur, its unique coat and unusual, pale green eyes.

Comparative adjectives compare two nouns. Add **er** to one-syllable adjectives (like *shy*).

A snow leopard is shyer than a mountain goat.

Add the word **more** or the word **less** before the adjective if the adjective has two or more syllables (like *beautiful*).

A snow leopard is more beautiful than a mountain goat.

Superlative adjectives compare three or more nouns. Add **est** to one-syllable adjectives. Add **most** or **least** for adjectives of two or more syllables.

The snow leopard is the shyest animal. It is the most beautiful animal.

Watch out for exceptions.

good $\longrightarrow$ better $\longrightarrow$ the best

bad $\longrightarrow$ worse $\longrightarrow$ the worst

FACT FILE

Animal:	Snow leopard
Habitat:	Central Asian mountains
Weight:	27 to 54 kg
Lifespan:	10 to 12 years
Diet:	Livestock, hares and birds

WILD FACT

Snow leopards are hunted for their beautiful, warm fur and for their organs, which are used in traditional Chinese medicine.

Task 1   Underline the adjectives in these sentences.

a The beautiful leopard had a light grey coat with ringed, black spots.

b Can you hear that growling, hissing sound behind that large rock?

c The ravenous snow leopard pounced on the unsuspecting sheep.

d The angry herder shouted at the leopard with a loud cry.

Task 2   Choose an adjective from the box. Change it into a comparative and insert it into a suitable sentence.

common	bad	loud	high

a A leopard's growl is _____ than a goat's bleat.

b That mountain top is much _____ than the forest below.

c The black leopard is _____ than the rare snow leopard.

d This terrible weather is _____ than yesterday.

Task 3   Underline the superlative adjectives in each sentence.

a The snow leopard was the most beautiful animal at the zoo.

b It would be the worst outcome if snow leopards became extinct.

c My least favourite animal at the zoo was the mountain viper.

d That is the tallest mountain I have ever seen!

WILD FACT
Snow leopards cannot roar, but they make other sounds like growling, chuffing, hissing and meowing.

Exploring Further ...

Use a thesaurus to help you find some exquisite adjectives to describe this snow leopard cub.

_____

_____

_____

_____

_____

Now leap to the pages 44–45 to record what you have learned in your explorer's logbook.

9

Pronouns

Pronouns are short words that **replace** nouns or **relate** to nouns.

Personal pronouns replace nouns to avoid repetition. (I, me, you, she, her, he, him, it, we, us, they, them)

Orangutans have long arms and they use them to move through trees.

Possessive pronouns show who or what owns something. (my, your, her, his, its, our, their, mine, yours, ours, theirs)

Orangutans use their hands and feet to swing through trees.

Relative pronouns link a relative clause to another part of a sentence. (that, which, who, whom, whose, whoever)

The forest that was home to many animals was being destroyed.

Demonstrative pronouns point out a specific thing. (this, these, that, those).

This orangutan / those orangutans.

WILD FACT

Orangutan means 'man of the forest'. They spend their lives climbing and swinging through the trees of dense rainforests. Sadly, the forests are being destroyed by humans, and so there are fewer and fewer of these wonderful apes left in the wild.

Task 1 — Circle the pronouns in these sentences.

a It has long, powerful arms.

b They are very intelligent like us.

c We travelled to Asia to see them.

d They sleep in nests in the trees.

FACT FILE

Animal:	Orangutan
Habitat:	The rainforests of Sumatra and Borneo
Weight:	33 to 82 kg
Lifespan:	30 to 40 years
Diet:	Fruits, leaves, bark, nuts, seeds, insects and honey

Task 2 — Circle the most suitable pronoun from the choices given.

a Orangutans are clever; <u>we / they / he</u> use leaves as umbrellas.

b The orangutan is arboreal, meaning <u>it / I / she</u> lives in trees.

c <u>Them / Those / They</u> orangutans are amazing!

d A mother orangutan cares for <u>its / his / her</u> babies for at least five years.

Task 3 — Think of a suitable pronoun to replace the underlined noun in these sentences. Write the pronoun on the line.

a <u>Greg's</u> favourite animal is an orangutan.

_____

b <u>Orangutans</u> need to be protected.

_____

c <u>The baby orangutan</u> clung to its mother.

_____

d <u>Orangutans</u> are the slowest breeding of all the primates.

_____

WILD FACT

One of the family! These great apes share 96% of our genes and are highly intelligent – they use leaves as umbrellas!

Exploring Further ...

Find the 8 hidden pronouns:

her
him
our
she
their
them
they
your

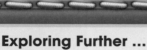

M	W	J	G	Y	U	E	R
E	S	T	O	T	O	E	Q
H	D	H	H	U	H	U	T
T	I	E	E	C	R	O	R
D	I	G	I	C	D	P	M
R	H	A	F	K	H	I	M
T	H	E	Y	S	Q	X	W
Y	D	Y	K	P	O	T	B

Now swing to pages 44–45 to record what you have learned in your explorer's logbook

Prepositions and articles

Prepositions show the relationship of one thing to another.

Some common prepositions are:
after, in, before, across, on, under, inside, along and **through**.

The black rhino loves to wallow <u>in</u> mud, find shade <u>under</u> rocks and trees and run fast <u>across</u> the African plains.

Determiners are used with nouns to help to identify things.

The most common determiners are **the**, **a** and **an**, (also known as articles).

The **definite article** is **the**.

The **indefinite article** is **a** (used before a consonant: *a black rhino*) or *an* (used before a word beginning with a vowel or a silent **h** (*an elephant* / *an hour*.)

Task 1   Underline the prepositions in these sentences.

a   The angry rhino charged through the bushes.

b   It leaves its scent along paths.

c   Before dawn, the rhinos gathered at the waterhole.

d   The warm sun rose over the African plains.

e   The oxpecker bird travels on the rhino's back.

WILD FACT
Don't try and outrun a rhino! They can reach speeds of 34mph – that's faster than Usain Bolt!

Task 2 Circle the indefinite articles in these sentences.

a The black rhino is an endangered animal.

b It is a very fast runner.

c A mother rhino uses her horn to warn off the hyenas.

Task 3 Tick the sentences that use correct articles.

a The rhino slept under an tree. ☐

b After running fast, the rhino rested by the waterhole. ☐

c The poacher followed the rhino along the path. ☐

d A oxpecker bird relaxed on the rhino's back. ☐

e That rhino has a very big horn above its nose. ☐

Now write the six prepositions used in the sentences above.

_____

Exploring Further ...

Use the words in the rhino's tummy to complete the sentence below.

sleepy a the
tree in under
sat shade rhino
the

After charging across the plains, _____

_____

Excellent work! Now charge to pages 44–45 to record what you have learned in your explorer's logbook.

13

Vibrant verbs

A **verb** describes an **action** (like hopping or croaking) or a state of **being** (am, is, are, was, were). Every sentence must contain a verb, otherwise it is not a sentence.

Verbs change **tense** to let us know if something happens in the present, past or future.

Present: *The frog hops through the forest.*

Past: *The frog hopped through the forest.*

Future: *The frog will hop through the forest.*

Modal verbs express necessity, uncertainty, ability or permission. The main modal verbs are:

will, would, can, could, may, might, shall, should, must *and* **ought**.

A predator might die if it licks a dart frog.   Less certain

A predator should die if it licks a dart frog.   ↓

A predator will die if it licks a dart frog.   More certain

It should have killed its prey.

Task 1	Circle the verb which makes the most sense.

a Their brilliant colours <u>alert / hide / amuse</u> predators.

b They <u>drop / capture / lose</u> their prey with their sticky tongues.

c Blowguns are <u>fired / cleaned / dipped</u> in poison.

d There <u>are / is / were</u> enough venom to kill ten men.

Task 2 Colour in the leaves that have a verb written on them.

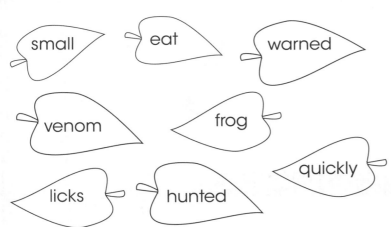

small eat warned venom frog quickly licks hunted

WILD FACT

Bright, beautiful but BEWARE! Poison dart frogs are extremely poisonous. Their vibrant colou startle potential predators ar warn them to keep away. Or lick of a poison dart frog an the predator will become very sick!

Task 3 Write a sentence using each of the modal verbs in the box.

shall	should	can	must	will

a _____

b _____

c _____

d _____

e _____

Exploring Further ...

Unscramble each anagram to make a verb.

PLEESING _____

NINGIGS _____

GINLICK _____

KRINNDIG _____

MILNIGS _____

MINGWIMS _____

Now hop to pages **44–45** to record what you have learned in your explorer's logbook.

Arctic adverbs

An **adverb** tells us more about a verb and often (but not always) ends in **ly**.

The polar bear's light fur blends easily with the snow.

     ↑   ↑

    verb adverb

An **adverbial phrase** is a group of words that also tells us more about a verb. These phrases tell us **where, when, how, why, with whom, how long or how often** something is done.

When	*The polar bear hunted <u>yesterday morning</u>.*
How	*The polar bear hunted <u>with great skill</u>.*
Where	*The polar bear hunted <u>across the ice-covered waters of the Arctic</u>.*

FACT FILE

Animal:	Polar bear
Habitat:	Snow-covered land and sea ice within the Arctic Circle
Weight:	410 to 720 kg
Lifespan:	15 to 30 years
Diet:	Seals and carcasses of dead whales

Task 1   Choose the most suitable adverb to complete these sentences.

rapidly   viciously   furiously   noiselessly   carefully

a Polar bears fight _____ when competing for females.

b Global warming is destroying their habitat _____.

c Polar bears groom themselves _____ after a good meal.

d They creep up _____, taking their prey by surprise.

e If polar bears lose their prey, they get angry and kick the snow _____.

16

Task 2 Draw a line from the start of the sentence to the most appropriate adverbial phrase.

a The powerful polar bear swam   from time to time.

b The cub waited for its mother   across the deep ocean.

c Polar bears may eat each other   with great patience.

Task 3 Write an adverbial phrase at the start of each sentence.

Example: <u>With his sharp teeth</u>, the polar bear devoured his prey.

a _____, Hettie read the book about the Arctic.

b _____, the baby seal tried to swim away.

c _____, the mother bear whacked her cub.

WILD FACT

Polar bear cubs stay with their mothers for over two years. They learn to 'freeze' when their mother is hunting and if they move she gives them a whack on the head!

WILD FACT

Polar bear fur is not actually white – it is colourless. It looks white because, like snow, it reflects the light. Depending on the time of year, bears can look yellow, brown or even green because of the algae growing in their hair!

Exploring Further ...

Find the words in this 'adverb spiral', which show how the mother cares for her cub. There are 11 words or phrases to find.

enthusiastically willingly fondly gently lovingly with ease peacefully devotedly merrily happily with good grace

Now stalk to pages 44–45 to record what you have learned in your explorer's logbook.

Expanding noun phrases

FACT FILE

Animal:	Black spider monkey
Habitat:	The tropical rainforests of South and Central America, and Mexico
Weight:	6 kg
Lifespan:	22 years
Diet:	Spiders, bird eggs, fruits, leaves and nuts

If you want to climb above the rest, give your writing a good stretch! How? By expanding **noun phrases**.

A **phrase** is a small group of words (or sometimes just one word) that forms part of a sentence.

In noun phrases, a noun (or pronoun) is the main word.

The spider monkey ⟶ *The wide-eyed spider monkey*

Expand noun phrases by adding:

Adjectives

The monkey clung to the tree. ⟶ *The <u>black-handed</u> monkey clung to the tree.*

Prepositional phrase

The monkey clung to the tree. ⟶ *The monkey clung to the tree <u>in the forest</u>.*

Adverbial phrase

The monkey clung to the tree. ⟶ *The monkey clung to the tree <u>really tightly</u>.*

Task 1   Expand these noun phrases with first an **adjective** and then a **prepositional phrase**.

Hint: you could start your prepositional phrases with some of these words:

through   **over**   **on to**   **behind**

a The _____ spider monkeys screeched _____.

b The _____ spider monkey leapt _____.

c The _____ spider monkey clung _____.

d The _____ spider monkey hid _____.

Task 2 Choose an ending for each sentence to expand the noun phrase. Draw a line to join the two parts.

a Sonny pulled a monkey face   until his mother fed him.

b Charlie swung like an ape   to South America next year.

c The hungry baby howled loudly   on the monkey bars in the park.

d I would love to travel   in the bathroom mirror.

Task 3 Tick the sentence that uses an **adverbial phrase** to give more detail about **how** the monkey moved.

a The spider monkey swings.   ☐

b The spider monkey swings as quick as a flash.   ☐

c The clever spider monkey swings through the forest trees.   ☐

WILD FACT
Spider monkeys get their name from their long, spidery limbs. Their tails helps them to balance and to reach things that are high up. It's like having an extra arm!

WILD FACT
You wouldn't want to live next to a troop of spider monkeys. They can produce screams and sobbing sounds, and they even bark when they are threatened.

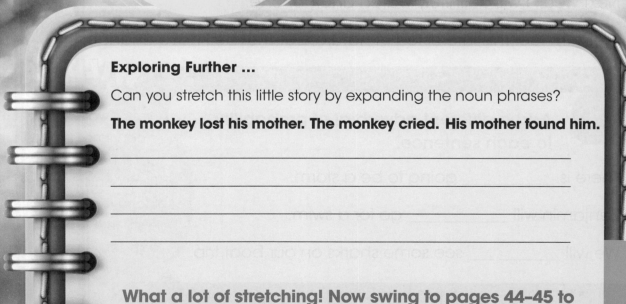

Exploring Further ...

Can you stretch this little story by expanding the noun phrases?

The monkey lost his mother. The monkey cried. His mother found him.

_____

_____

_____

_____

What a lot of stretching! Now swing to pages 44–45 to record what you have learned in your explorer's logbook.

19

Adverbials

Adverbials tell us extra information about the time, frequency and probability of an action.

Adverbials of time – tell us **when** an action or a state happens.

Yesterday, the shark was swimming in the shallow waters, and now he is there again.

Adverbials of frequency – tell us **how often** an action or state happens.

The shark can often be seen in the shallow waters but rarely comes close to the beach.

Adverbials of probability – tell us **how likely** it is that the action or state will happen.

The shark will certainly swim in the shallow waters, and you will possibly see him.

Task 1 — Circle the adverbials of time, frequency or probability in these sentences.

a I occasionally swim in the sea but usually prefer the swimming pool.

b Recently, I watched a film about sharks.

c Next week I will definitely watch another one.

d I seldom feel this interested in nature, but maybe I have changed.

Task 2 — Add a different adverbial of probability to each sentence.

a There is _____ going to be a storm.

b Benjamin will _____ go for a swim.

c We will _____ see some sharks on our boat trip.

beautifully

soon

very

seldom

maybe

quickly

honestly

after a while

possibly

sometimes

yesterday

WILD FACT

Open wide! Great white sharks have around 300 teeth, which grow in several rows.

WILD FACT

Shark attacks on humans are extremely rare. Sharks aren't really interested in us! Once they discover that you're a bony person and not a fat-filled seal, they'll swim off pretty quickly.

Exploring Further ...

Complete this crossword.

Across

3. Electro receptors can sense this.

5. It can smell a single drop of this.

6. Favourite food of the great white shark.

Down

1. Another name for 'killer'.

2. Sharks have several rows of these.

4. They don't have these to protect their eyes.

Now write your own sentence about great white sharks, using one or two adverbials of time, frequency or probability.

_____

_____

Excellent work! Now glide to pages 44–45 to record what you have learned in your explorer's logbook.

Complex sentences

Complex sentences contain one **main clause** (which makes sense on its own) and at least one **subordinate clause** (which does not make sense on its own).

A subordinate clause can come **before** or **after** the main clause, or even **in the middle**.

After he had waited patiently, the tiger pounced on his prey.

The tiger pounced on his prey after he had waited patiently.

The tiger, after he had waited patiently, pounced on his prey.

A complex sentence can also contain **more than one subordinate clause**.

After he had waited patiently, the tiger, that had stalked through the forest all night, pounced on his prey.

Task 1   Underline the main clause in each sentence.

a If the Bengal tiger loses its teeth, it can no longer kill prey and will starve to death.

b The tiger population is declining mainly because man is destroying their habitat.

c Although you might like to stroke their orange and black fur, their fearless eyes say it all.

d Because it is so large and powerful, the Bengal tiger has no natural predators.

e The tiger, when it is happy, squints its eyes.

FACT FILE

Animal:	Bengal tiger
Habitat:	The tropical rainforests and mangroves of South Asia
Weight:	109 to 227 kg
Lifespan:	8 to 10 years
Diet:	Birds, monkeys, boars, wolves and antelope

Task 2 For each sentence is the main clause (**M**) or the subordinate clause (**S**) underlined?

a <u>Using their coats as camouflage</u>, they lie in the shadows. ☐

b <u>They tend to hunt at night</u>, when humans are asleep. ☐

c Although cats don't usually like water, <u>tigers are strong swimmers</u>. ☐

d The white Bengal tiger, which has blue eyes, <u>is very rare</u>. ☐

Task 3 Write two **complex sentences** of your own about the Bengal tiger. Try to vary where you put the subordinate clause.

a _____

_____

b _____

_____

WILD FACT
There are 36 species of cat in the world and tigers are the largest.

WILD FACT
Unless humans do something to help, the tiger could become extinct. The world has lost a staggering 97 per cent of its wild tigers. Only an estimated 3200 remain.

Exploring Further ...

Can you solve this 'complex' brain teaser?

A man is walking down the village road with a tiger, a goat and a bundle of grass. Soon he arrives at the river bank, where there is one tiny boat that can only carry him and one animal or the bundle of grass at a time. It is too cold for any of them to swim, so the man has to make an important decision.

Here is the problem: Left alone, the tiger will eat the goat. Similarly, the goat will eat the grass bundle. How is the man going to take all three across the river safely?

Now pounce to pages 44–45 to record what you have learned in your explorer's logbook.

23

Standard English

Here are two important word sums for you:

Formal language + correct grammar and punctuation + varying sentence types = **Standard English**.

Informal language + double negatives + slang or colloquial language = **non-standard English**.

A news report is likely to contain Standard English.

 Good morning. Would you please tell us more about this fascinating animal? It is quite different to how we imagined it would be.

A conversation with a friend uses non-standard English.

 Hey! You gotta fill me in on this well cool animal! It ain't nothing like I thought it'd be.

WILD FACT

The blue whale can be as long as three double-decker buses. Its tongue weighs as much as an elephant; its heart as much as a car!

FACT FILE

Animal: Blue Whale
Habitat: Almost all the world's oceans
Weight: 181 437 kg
Lifespan: 80 to 90 years
Diet: Small crustaceans called krill

Task 1 Which is which? Write **S** for Standard English and **NS** for non-standard English in the boxes.

a I ain't never seen nothing so big!

b The blue whale is the largest animal on Earth.

c It don't have no teeth.

d Instead of teeth it has bristles.

e It's proper cold in the Atlantic Ocean.

Task 2

One of these sentences uses Standard English. Tick the correct sentence.

a You should of been here today. ☐

b You wasn't here today. ☐

c You was nowhere today. ☐

d You should have been here today. ☐

WILD FACT

Although we can't hear them, blue whales are one of the loudest animals on the planet. They use low-frequency pulses and groans and can hear each other 1500 kilometres away!

Task 3

Write the Standard English version of these sentences. Look out for the double negatives!

a The blue whale ain't got no teeth.

_____

b Them little fish don't have no chance of staying alive.

_____

c I shouldn't of stayed at home 'coz I could've seen the whales.

_____

Exploring Further ...

Rewrite this informal sentence in formal language, using the words in the whale.

I'm a well good swimmer 'coz I can do loads of kilometres and don't need no air for ages!

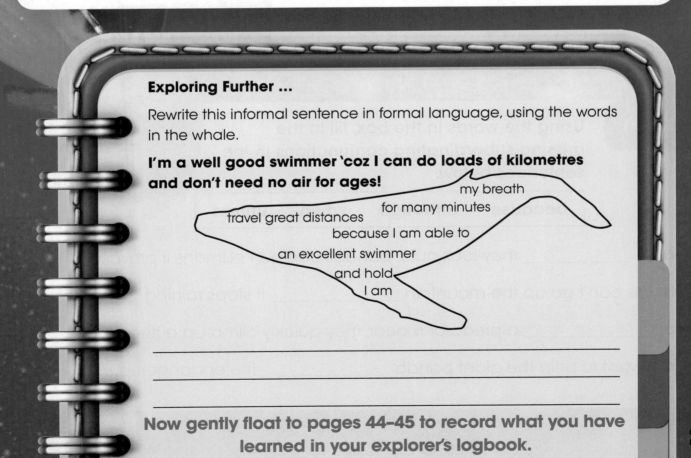

my breath
for many minutes
travel great distances
because I am able to
an excellent swimmer
and hold
I am

_____

_____

Now gently float to pages 44–45 to record what you have learned in your explorer's logbook.

25

Making connections

When they are born, baby pandas bond with their mothers – they have a **connection**. Our writing also needs to connect. That's why we use **connectives**. They have the important job of **linking** words, clauses, phrases and even sentences together.

There are three main types of connectives.

Connecting adverbs link clauses or sentences (to contrast, sequence or summarise ideas):

however   also   furthermore   finally   such as

Coordinating conjunctions link words, phrases or two main (independent) clauses:

for   and   nor   but   or   yet   so

Remember these with the acronym FANBOYS.

Subordinating conjunctions link a subordinate (dependent) clause to a main clause:

because   although   if   unless   when   until

FACT FILE

Animal:	Giant panda
Habitat:	Remote bamboo forests in Central China
Weight:	75 to 125 kg
Lifespan:	14 to 20 years
Diet:	Mainly bamboo

WILD FACT

Paws for thought. Did you know, pandas have five fingers and a large wrist bone that looks like a thumb? That's like having six fingers!

Task 1

Using the words in the box, fill in the missing subordinating conjunctions in the sentences below.

because	although	when	unless

a _____ they look cute, pandas can hurt humans if provoked.

b We can't go up the mountain _____ it stops raining.

c _____ a predator is near, they quickly climb up a tree.

d I want to help the giant panda _____ it is endangered.

Task 2 Underline the coordinating conjunction in each sentence.

a Giant pandas have powerful jaws and strong teeth.

b They live in mountains, but they once lived in the lowlands.

c The baby panda cried, so its mother gave it some food.

d Pandas eat bamboo or other plants.

WILD FACT

Giant pandas once lived in lowland areas but farming, forest clearing and other development has meant that they are now restricted to the mountains.

Task 3 Tick the examples that contain a connecting adverb.

a Giant pandas are beautiful. However, don't try to pat one. ☐

b Giant pandas are endangered. We should protect them. ☐

c Polar bears eat seals. In contrast, giant pandas eat bamboo. ☐

d They need a lot of food. Consequently, they eat all day. ☐

Exploring Further ...

Rearrange the letters to find a hidden word. The clues will help you.

Clue	Letters	Answer
Giant pandas have five of these.	GEFNIRS	_____
If pandas eat too quickly, they may get this	INTDIGSEION	_____
Another word for chew	NILBEB	_____
Pandas eat all day so have a very big one of these	PPAETIET	_____
Watch out for this predator!	LEDPAOR	_____
They used to live here	LALOWNSD	_____
The mothers do this when they are sleepy	YWNA	_____

Now take the first letter of each of the words, to make a final connective.

Write it here: _____

Now munch to pages 44–45 to record what you have learned in your explorer's logbook.

Active and passive

Sentences can be in the **active** or **passive** voice.

Active voice ⟶ *The gorilla ate the leaves.*

In this sentence, the focus is on the **gorilla**. It is the **subject** and it is doing the action. The leaves are the **object**.

Passive voice ⟶ *The leaves were eaten by the gorilla.*

In this sentence, the focus is on the **leaves**. They are the subject and the action is done to them. The gorilla is the object.

The sentences in the examples above describe the same thing but from different points of view.

FACT FILE

Animal:	Mountain gorilla
Habitat:	Volcanic mountains in Central Africa
Weight:	135 to 220 kg
Lifespan:	35 years
Diet:	Bark, roots, flowers, leaves, stems, fruit and small invertebrates

WILD FACT

The biggest and oldest male gorillas are known as 'silverbacks' because of the grey hairs on their back. Silverbacks can grow to 1.8 metres tall and are as strong as 10 men!

Task 1 Which is which? For each sentence, write **P** for passive voice and **A** for active voice in the box.

a The gorilla pounded his huge chest. ☐

b The forest was destroyed by the fire. ☐

c A bed of leaves was built by the family. ☐

d The mountain was covered in dense forest. ☐

e The band of gorillas roamed the mountain. ☐

WILD FACT

The mountain gorilla is critically endangered because of hunting, disease, the illegal pet trade and the destruction of its forest habitat.

Task 2 Rewrite these sentences in the active voice.

a The tools were used by the gorillas.

_____

b Babies are carried around for three years by their mothers.

_____

c Mountain gorillas are threatened by habitat loss and hunters.

_____

Task 3 Join a box on the right to one on the left to form a sentence in the passive voice.

a | The gorilla was hunted | | by conservationists. |

b | The leaves were eaten | | by the poachers. |

c | Gorillas are protected | | by the gorillas. |

Exploring Further ...

Look at this photograph. Write two sentences – one in the active voice, one in the passive voice – to describe what you see.

Active: _____

_____

Passive: _____

_____

Now roam to pages 44–45 to record what you have learned in your explorer's logbook.

Fittingly formal

We can categorise language into two main styles.

Formal language always uses Standard English and has a matter-of-fact style. It can use:

- technical language
- complex sentences
- subjunctive forms (*If it were to swim* or *Were they to swim*)
- the passive voice.

Formal language can be seen in reports, official letters, reference books or an email to a head teacher.

Informal language usually has a chatty (colloquial) style. It can use:

- contractions (*I'm, can't*)
- question tags (*That's a turtle, isn't it?*)
- judgemental or emotive words to show feelings
- personal pronouns such as 'I' and 'you'
- short sentences.

Informal language can be seen in text messages, blogs, notes and emails to friends.

FACT FILE

Animal:	Leatherback sea turtle
Habitat:	All oceans except the Arctic and the Antarctic
Weight:	900 kg
Lifespan:	Up to 45 years
Diet:	Jellyfish

Task 1   Write in the boxes the letter **F** if formal language should be used and **I** if informal language should be used when communicating in these scenarios.

a   A news report about marine life. ☐

b   A letter to a conservation charity about protecting sea turtles. ☐

c   An email to a friend about your holiday. ☐

d   A blog about beach life. ☐

e   An information leaflet about endangered animals. ☐

Rewrite these informal sentences in a more formal tone.

a Watch out guys! There's a pretty big turtle behind you.

_____

b You've gotta see these sea turtles. They're so cool!

_____

c Don't go near the jellyfish, mate – they'll sting you.

_____

d Yeah, ok, I'll watch out. But the sea turtle's harmless, isn't it?

_____

WILD FACT

The leatherback is the only sea turtle not to have a shell. Instead, it has a rubbery skin, which is how it gets its name.

Task 3 Imagine that you have seen some sea turtles on your holiday. Write a **brief email** to your best friend telling her about it. Remember to use informal language.

_____

_____

_____

_____

Exploring Further ...

Search the internet for information about sea turtles. Can you find a sea turtle blog? What about a sea turtle charity? Or a news article about sea turtles?

List three of the websites and say whether formal or informal language is used on the site.

Website	Language
_____	_____
_____	_____
_____	_____

Now paddle to pages 44–45 to record what you have learned in your explorer's logbook.

Apostrophes

Apostrophes are punctuation marks used in two ways.

Apostrophes for contraction are used in informal writing where a letter or letters have been missed out to join two words.

A narwhal's tusk isn't quite what it seems: it's actually a tooth!

Apostrophes for possession are used to show something or somebody **belongs** to a person or thing.

If the owner is **singular**, add an apostrophe, then **s**:

A narwhal's tusk.

If the owner is **plural** and ends in an **s**, just add an apostrophe after the **s**:

These mammals' tusks.

Task 1

Place the possessive apostrophe in the correct place.

a The fishermens boats were brand new.

b A stranded seals fate is always sealed.

c Those narwhals squeals are deafening.

d That narwhals tusk is amazing!

Task 2 Replace the bold words with a suitable contraction.

a I **cannot** believe **they are** holding their breath for so long!

_____

b I **will not** eat raw blubber. **I am** not brave enough!

_____

c If their tusks are touching, it **does not** mean **they are** fighting.

_____

Task 3 Rewrite these sentences, adding apostrophes in the correct places.

a The mens' harpoon guns are very sharp.

_____

b I ca'nt find the Arctic on this map.

_____

c Charlottes picture of narwhals is great!

_____

Exploring Further ...

Each of these questions contains a word that has a possessive apostrophe. Underline the word and then write the answer.

a Which mythical creature does the narwhal's nickname come from?

_____

b Why is the narwhal said to be like a soldier's corpse?

_____

c The long projection on this whale's head is not a horn. What is it?

_____

Well done! Now plunge to pages 44–45 to record what you have learned in your explorer's logbook.

Inverted commas

Inverted commas (or **speech marks**) are used in direct speech to show what a speaker actually says.

Line 1   *'Is that a wolf?' I cried excitedly.*
Line 2   *Mum replied, 'No, it's an African wild dog.'*
Line 3   *'What an amazing coat,' I said, 'and big, round ears!'*

Look carefully where the punctuation is in the example above.

Lines 1 and 3 begin with **direct speech**, so we always put a question mark, exclamation mark or comma **before** we close the inverted commas.

Line 2 begins by telling us who is speaking, so we always put a comma before we open the inverted commas. Then a full stop, exclamation mark or question mark just before the final inverted commas.

Remember: start a new paragraph when a new person begins speaking. Start direct speech with a capital letter, except when speech is interrupted (like line 3). In **reported speech** there are no inverted commas because it does not show the actual words spoken.

Task 1   Which sentences are punctuated correctly? Tick two.

a   'Oh, no!' It's chasing the zebra, I cried. ☐

b   'How many toes does an African wild dog have?' I asked. ☐

c   Mum said 'Let's keep our distance. He looks a bit hungry.' ☐

d   'In that case,' I replied, 'we'll stay in the minibus!' ☐

Task 2

Add inverted commas and other correct punctuation to this conversation.

He looks like ice cream I joked

Ice cream my sister laughed with toffee sauce

Mum replied You two girls have wild imaginations

That's because he's an African *wild* dog we chorused happily

WILD FACT

African wild dogs are have large bat-like ears and their coats are patterned in shades of brown, black and cream – like chocolate-chip ice cream with toffee sauce!

Task 3

Change these sentences from direct speech to reported speech.

a 'Can I hold your hand, Mum, I'm a bit scared?' Matilda asked.

_____

_____

b Mum smiled and said, 'Don't worry, Matilda. I'll look after you.'

_____

_____

c 'I'm really excited,' shouted Tom, 'because Martin is coming with us!'

_____

_____

WILD FACT

Wild dogs differ from wolves and other dogs because they have four toes instead of five!

Exploring Further ...

Can you punctuate these 'knock knock' jokes correctly?

Knock, knock	Knock, knock	Knock, knock
Who's there	Who's there	Who's there
Sarah	Oliver	Bow
Sarah who	Oliver who	Bow who
Sarah dog in there with you	Oliver sudden my dog went crazy	Not bow who, bow wow

Now chase to pages 44–45 and record what you have learned in your explorer's logbook.

Colourful commas

Commas are important punctuation marks and we use them in four main ways.

To **separate items** in a list:

Monarch butterflies are poisonous to birds, mice, frogs and lizards.

To **separate extra information** in a sentence:

Monarch butterflies, which feed on milkweed, are poisonous to birds.

To **separate two clauses** in complex sentences:

After a bird has tasted a monarch, it will never go back for more.

To **clarify meaning** in sentences:

When eating butterflies, absorb milkweed. **X**
When eating, butterflies absorb milkweed. ✓

Remember, commas indicate that you need to take a **brief pause**.

Task 1   Insert commas in suitable places in these sentences.

a The bird swooped down swallowed the butterfly and then felt very ill.

b Once it is in a cocoon the caterpillar changes into a butterfly.

c Like all insects they have six jointed legs three body parts a pair of antennae compound eyes and an exoskeleton.

d After hatching the monarch butterfly sheds its skin four times.

e Milkweed which contains a toxic chemical is eaten by monarch larvae.

Task 2   Next to each sentence, write how many people are looking at photographs.

a   When they left Dad, Ben and Emily looked through their photographs. ☐

b   When they left, Dad, Ben and Emily looked through their photographs. ☐

WILD FACT

Why are monarchs orange? It's a warning colour so that predators know they are poisonous. Don't worry – they won't harm humans!

Task 3   Add commas to separate the clauses.

a   If it is very cold and wet monarchs can freeze to death.

b   Although it is fragile the monarch is dangerous to animals.

c   Milkweed is being destroyed so the monarch population is decreasing.

d   Whilst they are still in a cocoon they change into butterflies.

WILD FACT

The monarch butterfly is sometimes called the 'milkweed butterfly' because this flower is the only thing the larvae can eat.

Exploring Further ...

Insert commas in the correct place in the sentence below.

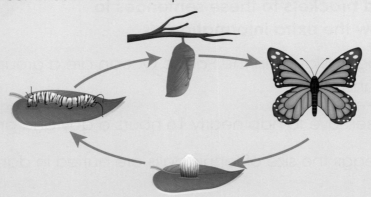

Monarch butterflies start out as an egg hatch into larvae wrap up in a cocoon and finally transform into a butterfly.

Now flutter to pages 44–45 to record what you have learned in your explorer's logbook.

Dashes – and brackets

The following sentence uses **dashes** and **brackets** to give extra information called **parenthesis**.

The Galápagos tortoise – also known as the giant tortoise – used to live in every continent (except Antarctica).

Brackets are also called **parentheses**. After the bracket, remember to use punctuation.

They used to live in every continent (except Antarctica).

      main information   parenthesis

If you want to give the extra information more emphasis, you can use dashes.

They used to live in every continent – except Antarctica.

If the extra information is in the middle of a sentence, two dashes are needed.

They used to live in every continent – except Antarctica – until they became extinct.

FACT FILE

Animal:	Giant tortoise
Habitat:	The Seychelles and Galápagos Islands
Weight:	Up to 300 kg
Lifespan:	100 years (or more)
Diet:	Grass, leaves and cacti

WILD FACT

Giant tortoises – large, tasty, and easy to kill – were quickly hunted to extinction anywhere where people lived. Now, only two groups remain – in the Seychelles and the Galápagos Islands.

Task 1   Add brackets to these sentences to show the extra information.

a   The Galápagos Islands in the Pacific Ocean are a group of volcanic islands.

b   Giant tortoises love to nap nearly 16 hours a day and graze.

c   Their large eggs the size of tennis balls are buried in damp sand or soil.

d   They love lying in mudholes especially on hot summer days.

Task 2   Add double dashes to show the parenthesis in these sentences.

a The Galápagos Islands named after the giant tortoises were discovered in 1535.

b Many unusual animals such as giant tortoises and iguanas live on these islands.

c Giant tortoises can survive a long time up to a year without eating or drinking.

Task 3   Tick the box if the sentence uses brackets correctly.

a Charles Darwin a great explorer (rode on the back of giant tortoises). ☐

b Charles (Darwin a great explorer) rode on the back of giant tortoises. ☐

c Charles Darwin (a great explorer) rode on the back of giant tortoises. ☐

d Charles Darwin a great explorer rode (on the back) of giant tortoises. ☐

Exploring Further ...

Search the facts that you have read to find a sentence (containing dashes) that is hidden in the tortoise's shell.

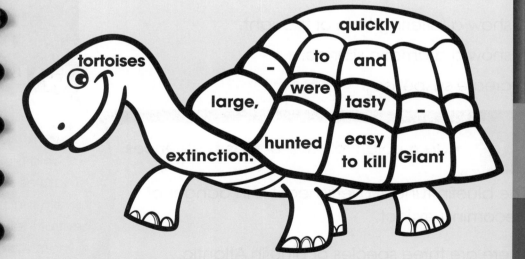

Write the sentence here.

_____

_____

Now amble to pages 44–45 to record what you have learned in your explorer's logbook.

39

Longer pauses

So that readers can really understand your writing, it is important to use a range of punctuation.

Colons indicate a long pause and are used:

- to introduce lists.
- to join two main clauses where the second explains the first.
- to introduce a quotation.

Semi-colons indicate a longer pause than a comma and are used:

- between clauses that could exist on their own but which are closely linked.
- to separate items in complex lists.

Ellipses (a row of three dots) are used:

- to show a pause.
- to show a faltering train of thought.
- to show a dramatic silence.
- to create suspense.

Task 1   Add a colon to each of these sentences.

a   The bluefin tuna is overfished it is in danger of becoming extinct.

b   There are three species of bluefin Atlantic, Pacific and Southern.

c   Tuna are fearsome predators they have the sharpest vision of any bony fish.

WILD FACT

Bluefin tuna can swim the Atlantic in 30 days!

FACT FILE

Animal: Bluefin tuna
Habitat: The Atlantic Ocean and the Mediterranean Sea
Weight: 250 kg
Lifespan: 15 years
Diet: Squid, eels, crustaceans and smaller fish

Task 2 Insert a semi-colon to separate two clauses.

a I like canned tuna I only eat yellowfin or skipjack.

b Bluefin tuna are warm-blooded most fish are not.

c Bluefin swim continuously if they stop they will die.

d Bluefin are built for speed they are torpedo-shaped.

Task 3 Add ellipses in suitable places in these sentences.

a The fish swam towards me I froze in fear.

b But the fish is harmless isn't it?

c I'd like to agree but

d We can stop the overfishing of tuna can't we?

Exploring Further ...

Julia is writing an opening to a short story, but it doesn't seem to make sense. Can you help her by adding **1 colon, 1 set of brackets, 1 semi colon ... and an ellipsis.**

As I swam in the vast ocean, I savoured the beauty around me the sparkling fish, the crystal blue water and the majestic shipwreck in the distance. The sun which was sinking below the horizon burned a brilliant orange. A bluefin tuna shot out of the water it left a glimmering trail. Suddenly, I felt something behind me

Now dive to pages 44–45 to record what you have learned in your explorer's logbook.

Quick test

Now try these questions. Give yourself 1 mark for every correct answer – but only if you answer each part of the question correctly.

1 **Underline the subordinate clause in this complex sentence:**
As the tiny mouse scuttled by, the king cobra shot at its prey.

2 **Tick the sentence with the correct verb form:**

The sea lions was lying together. ☐

The sea lions is lying together. ☐

The sea lions are lying together. ☐

3 **Circle all five nouns in this sentence.**
Since the elephants from India need to drink at least once a day, they are always close to a supply of water.

4 **Underline the comparative adjective.**
The snow leopard was stronger than the goat.

5 **Write a pronoun that could replace the underlined words in the sentence below.**
Each night, the girl's mother read <u>the girl</u> a story about wild animals in the jungle.

6 **Complete the sentence below with appropriate articles.**
It was _____ hungry lion we had seen yesterday, standing in front of _____ black rhino, giving _____ most terrifying of stares.

7 **Rewrite this sentence in the present tense.**
The unsuspecting snake swallowed the poison dart frog.

_____

8 **Add a suitable adverb to this sentence.**
The polar bear waited _____ for the seal to appear at the breathing hole.

9 **Add a prepositional phrase (beginning with through, beside or in) to expand this noun phrase.**
The black spider monkey swung happily _____

_____

10 **Complete this sentence with a suitable adverbial of probability.**
The baby seal will _____ die if it is spotted by a polar bear.

11 **Underline the main clause in this complex sentence.**

When it is hungry, the Bengal tiger stalks through the jungle.

12 **Rewrite this sentence in Standard English.**

It ain't fair that people won't stop hunting whales.

_____

13 **Circle the connective in the sentence below.**

Since pandas have powerful jaws, they are able to crush the tough bamboo.

14 **Rewrite this sentence in the passive voice.**

The gorilla smashed open the palm nut.

_____

15 **The sentence below uses informal language. True or false?**

Returning to the exact same spot where she herself was born, the mother sea turtle settled down to lay her eggs.

Answer: _____

16 **Change the underlined words to a contraction.**
Write the contraction in the box.

I have not heard of narwhals before.

17 **In which of these sentences is the question mark correctly used?**
Add a tick or a cross in the boxes.

'What do African wild dogs look like?' asked Teresa.

'What do African wild dogs look like'? asked Teresa.

'What do African wild dogs look like,' asked Teresa?

18 **Insert the missing comma in this sentence.**

The larva becomes a juicy colourful butterfly.

19 **Add a pair of brackets in the most suitable place in the sentence below.**

The giant tortoise the largest terrestrial reptile on Earth is nearing extinction.

20 **Insert a colon in the correct place in this sentence.**

There are many different types of tuna bluefin, skipjack and yellowfin.

How did you do?   1-5 Try again!   6-10 Good try!
11-15 Great work!   16-20 Excellent exploring!

/20

Explorer's Logbook

Tick off the topics as you complete them and then colour in the star.

Slithery sentences ☑

Naming nouns ☑

Arctic adverbs ☐

Colourful commas ☐

Vibrant verbs ☐

Complex sentences ☐

Expanding noun phrases ☐

Inverted commas ☐

Adverbials ☐

Standard English ☐

Apostrophes ☐

Exquisite adjectives ☐

Pronouns ☐

Active and passive ☐

Fittingly formal ☐

Dashes—and brackets ☐

Longer pauses ☐

Making connections ☐

Subject—verb agreement ☑

Prepositions and articles ☐

Answers

Pages 2–3

Task 1

a S **b** Q **c** C **d** S **e** E

Task 2

a Compound **b** Complex **c** Simple
d Complex

Task 3

Answers will vary. Accept any
grammatically correct clause:
a e.g. who quivered with fear.
b e.g. which were covered in cracks.
c e.g. who loved wild animals.

Exploring Further

a E **b** Q **c** S **d** C

Pages 4–5

Task 1

a Baby sea lions are called pups.
b Sharks and killer whales love to
   eat sea lions.
c A sea lion is able to hold its breath
   for 20 minutes.
d Sea lions have earflaps but seals
   don't.

Task 2

a was **b** were **c** is **d** are

Task 3

a devoured **b** is **c** lies **d** dive

Exploring Further

Answers will vary. Accept any
grammatically correct answers that
complement the images.

Pages 6–7

Task 1

a Elephants   mammals   land.
b trunks   trees   grass.
c herds   clans.
d joy   animals.

Task 2

Common	Proper	Collective	Abstract
elephant	Asia	herd	anger
ivory	India	clan	hope
mammal	Emily	crowd	hurt
mirror	Monday	flock	peace

Task 3

a their habitat is being destroyed to
   build roads, houses and farms.
b poachers are hunting them to sell
   their tusks, skin and meat.
c they are captured and sent to
   work in the timber industry.

Exploring Further

a ABSTRACT **b** COLLECTIVE
c COMMON **d** PROPER **e** HERD
f TUSK

Pages 8–9

Task 1

a beautiful, light grey, ringed, black
b growling, hissing, large
c ravenous, unsuspecting
d angry, loud

Task 2

a louder **b** higher **c** more common
d worse

Task 3

a most beautiful **b** worst
c least favourite **d** tallest

Exploring Further

Answers will vary. Accept any
suitable adjectives.

Pages 10–11

Task 1

a It **b** They, us **c** We, them **d** They

Task 2

a they **b** it **c** Those **d** her

Task 3

a His **b** They **c** It **d** They

Exploring Further

M	W	J	G	Y	U	E	R
E	S	T	O	T	O	E	Q
H	D	H	H	U	H	U	T
T	I	E	E	C	R	O	R
D	I	G	I	C	D	P	M
R	H	A	F	K	H	I	M
T	H	E	Y	S	Q	X	W
Y	D	Y	K	P	O	T	B

Pages 12–13

Task 1

a through **b** along **c** before, at
d over **e** on

Task 2

a an **b** a **c** A

Task 3

Correct sentences are **b c** and **e**.
Prepositions: under, after, by, along,
on, above

Exploring Further

After charging across the plains, the
sleepy rhino sat in the shade under
a tree.

Pages 14–15

Task 1

a alert **b** capture **c** dipped **d** is

Task 2

Verbs: eat, warned, licks, hunted

Task 3

Answers will vary. Accept any with
modal verb used correctly.

Exploring Further

SLEEPING, SINGING, LICKING,
DRINKING, SMILING, SWIMMING.

Pages 16–17

Task 1

a viciously **b** rapidly **c** carefully
d noiselessly **e** furiously

Task 2

a The powerful polar bear swam
   across the deep ocean.
b The cub waited for its mother with
   great patience.
c Polar bears may eat each other
   from time to time.

Task 3

Answers will vary. Accept any
grammatically correct adverbial
phrase.

Exploring Further

happily, merrily, devotedly, peacefully,
enthusiastically, willingly, fondly, gently,
lovingly, with good grace, with ease

Pages 18–19

Task 1

Answers will vary. Accept any
suitable adjective and prepositional
phrase. Example answers:
a The excited spider monkeys
   screeched through the trees.
b The hungry spider monkey leapt
   on to the branch.
c The frightened spider monkey
   clung on to its mother.
d The cheeky spider monkey hid
   behind the elephant.

Task 2

a Sonny pulled a monkey face in the
   bathroom mirror.
b Charlie swung like an ape on the
   monkey bars in the park.
c The hungry baby howled loudly
   until his mother fed him.
d I would love to travel to South
   America next year.

Task 3

Correct answer: **b**.

Exploring Further

Answers will vary. Example answer: The baby spider monkey lost his mother in the huge forest. The frightened monkey cried for a long time. After searching hard, his relieved mother found him next to a tall tree.

Pages 20–21

Task 1

a occasionally   usually   **b** Recently, **c** Next week

d seldom, maybe

Task 2

Answers will vary. Accept any appropriate adverbial of probability.

Task 3

after a while, yesterday, sometimes, possibly, seldom, soon, maybe

Exploring Further

Down: 1. predator; 2. teeth; 4. eyelids; Across: 3.heartbeat; 5. blood; 6. seal Sentence: Answers will vary. Accept any with appropriate adverbials.

Pages 22–23

Task 1

a it can no longer kill prey and will starve to death.

b The tiger population is declining

c their fearless eyes say it all.

d the Bengal tiger has no natural predators.

e The tiger squints its eyes.

Task 2

a S   **b** M   **c** M   **d** M

Task 3

Answers will vary. Accept any grammatically correct complex sentence.

Exploring Further

The man takes the goat with him to the other side first, leaves the goat and comes back to get the tiger. He then leaves the tiger on the other side and brings the goat back again. He leaves the goat there and takes the bundle of grass to the other side. He returns again to pick up the goat and, after crossing the river for a final time, he resumes his journey with the tiger, goat and bundle of grass!

Pages 24–25

Task 1

NS: **a**, **c**, **e**   S: **b**, **d**

Task 2

Correct answer: **d**.

Task 3

a The blue whale has no teeth. / does not have any teeth. / has not got any teeth.

b Those little fish do not have a chance of staying alive. / have no chance of staying alive.

c I should not have stayed at home because I could have seen the whales.

Exploring Further

I am an excellent swimmer because I am able to travel great distances and hold my breath for many minutes.

Pages 26–27

Task 1

a Although   **b** unless   **c** When **d** because

Task 2

a and   **b** but   **c** so   **d** or

Task 3

a, **b**, **c**

Exploring Further

FINGERS, INDIGESTION, NIBBLE, APPETITE, LEOPARD, LOWLANDS, YAWN, The connective is: FINALLY.

Pages 28–29

Task 1

A = **a**, **e**

P = **b**, **c**, **d**

Task 2

a The gorillas used the tools.

b The mothers carry their babies for three years.

c Habitat loss and hunters threaten the mountain gorillas.

Task 3

a The gorilla was hunted by the poachers.

b The leaves were eaten by the gorillas.

c Gorillas are protected by conservationists.

Exploring Further

Example answers:

Active: The mother cuddled her baby.

Passive: The baby was cuddled by its mother.

Pages 30–31

Task 1

F = **a**, **b**, **e**

I = **c**, **d**

Task 2

Answers will vary but should include

grammatically correct formal language. Example answers:

a Be careful everyone, there is a large turtle behind you.

b You must see these sea turtles. They are fascinating!

c Be sure to keep away from the jellyfish as they are very likely to sting.

d Yes, I will take care; however, is it not true that the sea turtle is harmless?

Task 3

Answers will vary but should be characterised by an informal tone containing contractions and short sentences.

Exploring Further

Answers will vary.

Pages 32–33

Task 1

a fishermen's   **b** seal's   **c** narwhals' **d** narwhal's

Task 2

a can't, they're   **b** won't, I'm

c doesn't, they're

Task 3

a The men's harpoon guns are very sharp.

b I can't find the Arctic on this map.

c Charlotte's picture of narwhals is great!

Exploring Further

a narwhal's / The unicorn

b soldier's / It floats belly up like a dead body

c whale's / A tooth

Pages 34–35

Task 1

Correct: **b**, **d**

Task 2

'He looks like ice cream,' I joked. Ice cream,' my sister laughed, 'with toffee sauce.'

Mum replied, 'You two girls have wild imaginations.' 'That's because he's an African wild dog!' we chorused happily.

Task 3

a Matilda asked her Mum if she could hold her hand because she was a bit scared.

b Matilda's Mum smiled and told her that she would look after her.

c Tom shouted with excitement because Martin was going with them.

Exploring Further

'Knock, knock!'
'Who's there?'
'Sarah!'
'Sarah who?'
'Sarah dog in there with you?'

'Knock, knock!'
'Who's there?'
'Oliver!'
'Oliver who?'
'Oliver sudden my dog went crazy.'

'Knock, knock!'
'Who's there?'
'Bow!'
'Bow who?'
'Not bow who, bow wow!'

Pages 36–37
Task 1
a The bird swooped down, swallowed the butterfly and then felt very ill.
b Once it is in a cocoon, the caterpillar changes into a butterfly.
c Like all insects, they have six jointed legs, three body parts, a pair of antennae, compound eyes and an exoskeleton.
d After hatching, the monarch butterfly sheds its skin four times.
e Milkweed, which contains a toxic chemical, is eaten by monarch larvae.

Task 2
a 2   b 3

Task 3
a If it is very cold and wet, monarchs can freeze to death.
b Although it is fragile, the monarch is dangerous to animals.
c Milkweed is being destroyed, so the monarch population is decreasing.
d Whilst they are still in a cocoon, they change into butterflies.

Exploring Further
Monarch butterflies start out as an egg, hatch into larvae, wrap up in a cocoon and finally transform into a butterfly.

Pages 38–39
Task 1
a The Galápagos Islands (in the Pacific Ocean) are a group of volcanic islands.

b Giant tortoises love to nap (nearly 16 hours a day) and graze.
c Their large eggs (the size of tennis balls) are buried in damp sand or soil.
d They love lying in mudholes (especially on hot summer days).

Task 2
a The Galápagos Islands – named after the giant tortoises – were discovered in 1535.
b Many unusual animals – such as giant tortoises and iguanas – live on these islands.
c Giant tortoises can survive a long time – up to a year – without eating or drinking.

Task 3
Correct answer: c.

Exploring Further
Giant tortoises – large, tasty and easy to kill – were quickly hunted to extinction.

Pages 40–41
Task 1
a The bluefin tuna is overfished: it is in danger of becoming extinct.
b There are three species of bluefin: Atlantic, Pacific and Southern.
c Tuna are fearsome predators: they have the sharpest vision of any bony fish.

Task 2
a I like canned tuna; I only eat yellowfin or skipjack.
b Bluefin tuna are warm-blooded; most fish are not.
c Bluefin swim continuously; if they stop they will die.
d Bluefin are built for speed; they are torpedo-shaped.

Task 3
a The fish swam towards me ... I froze in fear.
b But the fish is harmless ... isn't it?
c I'd like to agree but ...
d We can stop overfishing of bluefin tuna ... can't we?

Exploring Further
As I swam in the vast ocean, I savoured the beauty around me: the sparkling fish, the crystal blue water and the majestic shipwreck in the distance. The sun (which was sinking below the horizon) burned a brilliant orange. A bluefin tuna shot

out of the water; it left a glimmering trail. Suddenly, I felt something behind me ...

Answers to quick test
1 As the tiny mouse scuttled by, the king cobra shot at its prey.
2 The sea lions are lying together.
3 elephants, India, day, supply, water.
4 The snow leopard was stronger than the goat.
5 her
6 It was the hungry lion we had seen yesterday, standing in front of a / the black rhino, giving the most terrifying of stares.
7 The unsuspecting snake swallows / is swallowing the poison dart frog.
8 Accept any appropriate adverb, e.g. patiently, cautiously.
9 Accept any appropriate peropositional phrase, e.g. through the trees / beside his mother / in the forest.
10 Accept any appropriate adverbial of probability, e.g. surely, definitely, probably.
11 When it is hungry, the Bengal tiger stalks through the jungle.
12 It is unfair / not fair that people will not stop hunting whales / continue to hunt whales.
13 Since
14 The palm nut was smashed open by the gorilla.
15 False.
16 haven't.
17 First sentence is correct: 'What do African wild dogs look like?' asked Teresa.
18 The larva becomes a juicy, colourful butterfly.
19 The giant tortoise (the largest terrestrial reptile on Earth) is nearing extinction.
20 There are many different types of tuna: bluefin, skipjack and yellowfin.